Selected Poems of Sándor Csoóri

T0151995

Selected Poems
of Sándor Csoóri

TRANSLATED BY LEN ROBERTS

COPPER CANYON PRESS

The publication of this book was supported by grants from the National
Endowment for the Arts, the Washington State Arts Commission, and
the Lannan Foundation.

Copper Canyon Press is in residence with Centrum at Fort Worden State
Park.

Library of Congress Cataloging-in-Publication Data

Csoóri, Sándor.
    [Poems. Selections]
    Selected Poems of Sándor Csoóri / translated by Len Roberts.
      p. cm.
    ISBN 1-55659-047-4
      1. Csoóri, Sándor—Translations into English.   I. Roberts, Len,
    1947–   . II. Title.
    PH3213.C8145A26   1992   92-6972
    894'.51113—dc20

Acknowledgments

Agni: "I Have to Look Long."

The American Poetry Review (poems selected as part of a twenty-eight poem feature of Hungarian poetry): "Prophesying About Your Time," "Barbarous Prayer," "You're Rising and Vanishing," and "People, Boughs."

Chelsea: "Day by Day," "Sea Gull-Line," and "On the Third Day It Began to Snow."

Crab Creek Review: "I'd Rather Stay at Home" and "Memories of November."

Delos: "May Beetles" and "I Go Near You to Die."

Denver Quarterly: "This Day" and "The Poppy Clatters at Night."

Indiana Review: "Postponed Nightmare" and "The Day Has Passed."

International Poetry Review: "Farewell to Finland," "Apparition," "Esztergom Summer," "Winter's Voice Has Softened," and "Darkly from the Darkness."

Kenyon Review: "No Kin of Yours, Just a Friend" and "Somebody Consoles Me with a Poem."

The Literary Review: "A Drop of Blood on the Ground" and "Questions to Carriers of the Dead."

Mark: "The Nook Was Fine for Me" and "Only Myself Have I Not Seen."

Maryland Review: "Because There Was a Time" and "Blinding Map of Nothing."

Mid-American Review (poems selected as a chapbook of Hungarian poetry): "Everyday History," "On the Third Day the Snow Began to Fall," "A Thin, Black Band," "Dozing on the Train," and "Night Journey in Germany."

New England Review & Bread Loaf Quarterly: "Maple Leaf" and "Summer, with Halo."

Northwest Review: "Message."

Plainsongs: "Let the Timbrel Rattle," "Green Twig in My Hand," and "I Saw Your Face."

Poetry East: "Ague."

Poetry Miscellany: "Aiming Orb."

Prism International: "My Mother Is a Black Rose" and "I Believed Then."

Translation: "You, Hungry for the Sun" and "My Masters."

Visions International: "What Do You Envy Me" and "The Wind with Its Nerves."

My thanks to those who created the literal drafts of these poems, especially to László Vértes for his continual support and helpful advice. I am also grateful to the Soros and Witter Bynner Foundations for monetary grants which enabled me to continue my work, and to the Fulbright Commission for a translation award to Hungary.

Table of Contents

For Nancy, Joshua, Bradford, and Tammy

Introduction

Sándor Csoóri (born in Zámoly, Hungary in 1930), a leading contemporary Hungarian poet, essayist and scriptwriter, has been called "the genius of discontent," "the greatest writer in Hungarian intellectual life," "the gray eminence of the Good Cause," as well as the "national poet," one who has taken upon himself the responsibility of his nation's well-being, physical and spiritual. He is, without any doubt, the most prominent artistic spokesman for the Hungarian people. He has captured their hardships and struggles, as well as the accompanying sense of guilt and loss, which permeate his post-World War II generation. Without sacrificing his poetry to propaganda, he has been able, by absorbing the social and political turmoil of his period into himself, to digest these turmoils and re-create them on a personal, artistic level which is completely authentic.

Csoóri's identification of his own fate with that of his country's, places him in the Hungarian mainstream literary tradition called *Fate-literature,* a tradition which stems from Sándor Petőfi, whose rousing poem of revolt helped to ignite the Hungarian Revolution of 1848, and János Arany, also of the nineteenth century. This literary mainstream continued in the twentieth century with such writers as Endre Ady and Gyula Illyés during the 1920s, 1930s and 1940s, and it survived during the post-World War II years in such poets as Ferenc Juhász and László Nagy, with Csoóri being the major remaining representative of that school. In this literary tradition, the poet is the conscience and teacher of his country, both in his public and his personal poems, and he assumes the moral responsibility for verbalizing the problems of the Hungarian people and of humankind.

One of these problems is the loss, in the Modernist period, of the past's great Hungarian leaders, those who upheld the traditional values of the country, who, as Csoóri says, held "Hungary's broken peony in their hands." In his poem, "My Masters," which appeared in *The World's Monuments* (1989), he dramatically presents this loss when he asks, "Where, where are my masters?"

> In the past they'd appear without even being called.
> They'd come before the first peal of the bells,
> across barren yards: madmen, poets,
> alcoholic saints; they'd come from the night's marshes,
> holding Hungary's broken peony in their hands.

But Csoóri, and presumably the Hungarian people for whom he speaks, can no longer find their "masters":

> Where might they linger now? Where might they be kept
>   waiting?
> With whom do they share their deaths,
> the way prisoners of war share a lone potato?
> As though they are ashamed
> of this fouled landscape that's sunk into itself,
> and their dirtied mission.

Accompanying this sense of loss is a great sense of self-betrayal, for Csoóri insists it is the individual's responsibility to retain integrity in the face of the depersonalizing modernist and socialist society. And, to Csoóri, self-betrayal is country-betrayal, for he believes that self and country are indistinguishable. In another, recent poem, "Day by Day," he connects this self-betrayal with the "coy dictatorships" of his era:

> Oh, coy dictatorships, what a tale this is!
> We wear down, lose vitality, molder away like silk,
>   and he who would have betrayed Christ long ago,
> now, without batting an eyelid, day by day betrays himself,
> great beasts play with his heart,
>   like clawed pussycats with a ball of yarn.

In the midst of this loss and betrayal, it is the poet's task to speak for his people, to remind them of their community's past,

4

of their heritage. This is a nearly impossible task, Csoóri admits in the last stanza of the poem, although he is speaking for his people even in the admission:

> Lying on his back, the poet keeps trying to sing
> out on the hilltop, but he's lost
> > his tongue.
> The taste of spoiled elegies rises again in his mouth,
> as though he'd been fed
> > the livers of infected birds at dusk.

One of the poet's tasks in such times is to catalog the defeats as well as the few successes of his people; it is his job to hear the oppressed, the voices of those who suffered and died. Csoóri's poetry is filled with ghosts who come back insistently to remind him that all is not well. As Csoóri says in "The Day Has Passed," a poem which appeared in the volume *A Green Twig in My Hand* (1985), "for a long time the distant dead look/today, still, from under the rubble,/as though I had died in the street fighting instead of them/and the victors now trampled over me."

Csoóri, as poet in the Fate-literature tradition, must account for the state of Hungary during and after World War II, a world of toppled bridges, razed villages, the wounded and dead, as well as those who survived the last forty-five years in silence. These war images gain even more power and significance when one realizes that Hungarians were not permitted, for the past forty-five years, to talk, let alone write about Hungary's role during World War II. Those soldiers and civilians who died were not officially mourned nor publicly remembered until very recently. "The chronic memory of violence," as he calls it, appears again and again in his poems. A tremendously vivid image in "A Dawn Story," which probably recalls the days of his youth when he returned to his village to bury the dead, portrays what seems a typical nightmare:

This night of mine was the devil's again.
In water up to my ankles, I dug a big ditch.
From its yellow, mud walls
molding tatters of clothing stuck out:
a shirtsleeve and a coat,
and, crooked, a dead man's brimmed hat.

Later in the poem, as the speaker tries to run away from the brutal vision, he realizes that "people were slaughtered here as a circus spectacle," and he concludes the poem by saying "this country is not my country anymore,/beyond the forest, reed-beds are reddening,/and beyond them, endless water, thundering nothing."

Csoóri's love-hate relationship with his country creates a dense, ambivalent texture in many of his poems, for there is a constant argument going on within the man and his work: Should I leave or should I not? In actuality, though, there is no question of Csoóri's leaving, for he knows he is bound to his country, both in his (its) ruin and in his (its) healing. He acknowledges this openly in "The Wind with Its Nerves," an early poem:

Here your hand turns blue
and here your cymbal-face claps to the ground.

There is no other age which would harbor you,
no other country which would give you a name:
here you are bound
by the nerves of the wind,
by the cotton threads of the fog,
here you are welded by the greatest patience.

He is, truly, "bound" by his country, and it is no coincidence that he ends this poem with figures of speech from the war:

Like a piece of shrapnel rambling in your flesh,
you carry its ruins within yourself;

and if your wounding binds you here,
your healing binds you here, too.
Lie down in the mud,
in the harrow-rough thornbed,
laugh or snarl –
You can embrace somewhere else as well,
but only here does the right to kill remain for you.

In his poems, Csoóri is continually searching for answers to the existential problems he and his countrymen confront, sometimes in the face of a beautiful woman, in an attachment to nature, or in the doggedly persistent belief in the value of the search itself. But his poetry usually does not provide answers; it just presents, dramatically, the dilemmas found. His speaker typically is alone, remembering a past that once held meaning, considering a future which, at best, will be filled with struggle and more death. The present, under Csoóri's unrelentingly honest gaze, is one of lies and hypocrisy, a time in which the speaker is barely able to maintain his own integrity. He dramatically contrasts the search for truth he believes existed in the past with the lies of those living in the present in a recent poem, "The Missed Roads":

I searched for the cemeteries that had been carried off and I
made the dead speak, whisper from beneath the earth
about the heads severed by axes, since it's true now
that barren, raw chalk creaks in the mouths of the living
instead of words. . . .

Thus, it is the individual's responsibility to distinguish between what is true and what is not. But in a society which fosters falsehood and subversion of the self, this becomes a most difficult and existential task, for the individual in his works must rely primarily upon himself for the answers — if there are any. And, as Csoóri has said, the individual must attempt this without any hope for success: "Because hopelessness: is self defense, the source of final calmness. And without that, how could anyone act? In other words, the Eastern European is not only doomed to existence, but also to existentialism, because he can preserve his sanity and honesty only through the conscious or instinctive undertaking, or perhaps the religion, of hopeless action."

Yet one of the major strengths of Csoóri's work is that it presents an individual who *is* able to exist, albeit with extreme hardships, in an age and society which value the depersonalization of man. Csoóri's speaker is always an identifiable person (presumably himself), one with a past (however horrific), a present (however despondent), and a future (however tenuous); this is the voice of a human being struggling to maintain independent individuality. Csoóri has said, "From the first, there has been present in my work, in whichever genre, a general sense of unease about how to maintain the existence of the human personality in the world amid the great campaigns of depersonalization." ("Autobiographical Note," *Arion* 12, Budapest, 1980.) Csoóri has refused to surrender this concept of selfhood, either to the "great campaigns of depersonalization" or to the abstractions of much contemporary poetry, thus he is considered an exemplary model for his fellow Hungarians.

One of his cultural weapons against this depersonalization is his insistence on the importance of traditional folk values. He believes that these values are integral to the Hungarian identity and he thus insistently resists their loss. It was Csoóri who linked the rural (peasant, folk) and urban traditions most successfully in his work, creating a synthesis between local and universal values which served as a bridge for the Hungarian who sought his roots and identity in his country's past. Images from Csoóri's peasant childhood, such as "my sunken village may be seen from here,/my child-sole's lacy print in the dust," lead him to conclude, "it's good to know who I was,/it's good to know who I am...."

A good example of the modern day "rudeness" intruding upon the traditional values of the past is seen in his very early and popular poem, "My Mother Is a Black Rose," in which he says, "My mother is rudely taunted/by upstart strangers./My mother, panicked,/stammers and gets hoarse," and, a line later, "let no one harm her any more,/or add to her fear." This shows the poet's awareness of the past's (and its values) fragility, as well as its inability to deal with a coarser present. The poem also shows the extreme poverty in which his mother, and most of her countrymen, must live: "My mother gets nowhere/although she keeps treading paths —/from the star of poverty/her forehead is cracked." This, the poet says, is the fate of those who live in the country, those who are forgotten, as are their values, by the urbanized, socialized population. Appropriately, the poem ends with an image from a folk-song, in which a bird comes to take the mother away:

My mother has a headache,
  nothingness pains her,
my mother is a black rose,
  she cannot put on new colors.
  One night she will crumple to the ground,
she'll be small, shattered —
  A bird will come to snap its beak
  and soar away with her.

In the first years following the Soviet "liberation" of Hungary, Csoóri believed, as did many members of his generation, in the great social experiment, and he even mentioned Rákosi, the communist dictator, favorably in an early poem. In 1951, however, when he returned from Budapest to his rural village, Zámoly, in western Hungary, he saw the extreme poverty and injustice which the new system had inflicted on his countrymen. They had been promised prosperity but everything they produced was taken by the authorities and, soon afterward, the forced collectivism began which destroyed the lives of many peasants. At this point, he began writing poems which he describes as less "entranced." His first book of poems, *The Bird Takes Wing*, 1954, contains poetry which is direct, lyrical description, following the model of Sándor Petófi. However, beginning with his next book, *Devil-Butterfly*, 1957, which Csoóri considers the recommencement of his political career, his poems begin to develop even more as Fate-literature and the poet assumes moral responsibility for the plight of his country. It is not until his next book, though, *Escape from Loneliness*, published in 1962, that he writes with the force and style that has characterized his poetry ever since. It was during this time that Csoóri read and was greatly influenced by other European poets, such as Federico García Lorca, Paul Éluard, and Pierre Reverdy, influences which showed in Csoóri's increasing surrealism and also in his more personal expression. These influences, coupled with his great interest in folk tales and their tremendous emphasis upon the image and seemingly surrealistic visions, created the more symbolic and visionary voice that characterizes all of Csoóri's later poetry.

It is not, however, the surrealistic techniques of the Europeans nor the folk tales of his own country which most influenced Csoóri, for his poetry has never been extremely surreal; instead, it has remained firmly embedded in sensual experience. Rather, it is these Europeans' reliance upon the direct representation of unfalsified reality (Reverdy especially), their use of folk tales and song, coupled with the strong use of the image (Endre Ady and Lorca especially), and their essential fusing of the personal and the public in their poetry (his Fate-literature precursors and Lorca and Éluard especially) which he immediately grafted onto his own poetry. In addition to these great influences, it is more than just coincidence that Reverdy's, Eluard's, and Lorca's poems are infused with man's perishability and ultimate death. This quality, which Lorca termed "duende," permeates Csoóri's writing. It is an inherent preoccupation with the full richness of man's existential state, including his suffering and death, and it may be seen in nearly every one of his poems.

Throughout his lifetime, in his poems, essays and filmscripts, Sándor Csoóri has served as a witness to his times, especially to Hungary's fate during World War II and its aftermath of Socialism. Although many of his poems are very grim, indeed, nightmarish, they are, in their essential moments, redeeming, for they represent man's spirit coming to terms with the hardships of existence. And it is this spirit of endurance which he exemplifies in his life and work, a spirit he bequeaths, as he says in "Prophesying about Your Time," to those who have suffered and waited:

> For your time shall come,
> you'll see, it shall come,...
> it shall be magnificent,
>   I tell you, it shall be magnificent,
> because it is only you who can come after them,
> you, who were able to wait
> from the first to the second pain,
> shifting from the red into the black,
> and from black back,
> and become incarnated every day,
> to sweat,
>   to split apart, to go on.

N O T E: The three sections of this volume present selections of Csoóri's poems in an approximate reverse chronological order, ranging from his most recent poems (1982 to the present), to poems written between 1973 and 1982 in Part Two, and, finally, to poems written between 1962 and 1973 in Part Three.

All poems not otherwise noted have been translated solely by Len Roberts.

Part One

(1982 - PRESENT)

My Masters

Where, where are my masters?
In the past they'd appear without even being called.
They'd come before the first peal of the bells,
across barren yards: madmen, poets,
alcoholic saints; they'd come from the night's marshes,
holding Hungary's broken peony in their hands.

One of them would come with a flood,
another from between clattering tracks,
another limping, with the white frost of Bakony on his back.

And I always read the words
from their motionless lips.
Where might they linger now? Where might they be kept waiting?
With whom do they share their deaths,
the way prisoners of war share a lone potato?
As though they are ashamed
of this fouled landscape that's sunk into itself,
and their dirtied mission.

Day by Day

Day by day the thorns are sharper,
day by day July flashes more forebodingly,
        as if a monster
                had teeth made of gold.

He who has only sighed thus far, standing on his threshold,
now grinds a jaw even in his timid dream,
        throws plates to the ground
                and kicks cats lying in the sun,
because he wants to hear crying and harsh moans to comfort
                himself,
making the echoes of old miseries even louder.

The century is lessening, frightfully thinning,
there's a brown blotch on its bony Mephisto face.
Day by day the smile, locust blossom, and the dead one
        who fulfilled his mission are becoming stranger and
                        stranger to it,
and everything reaches its own glory in it
                only as a fragment.

Oh, coy dictatorships, what a story this is!
We wear down, lose vitality, molder away like silk,
        and he who would have betrayed Christ long ago,
now, without batting an eyelid, day by day betrays himself,
great beasts play with his heart,
                like clawed pussycats with a ball of yarn.

Lying on his back, the poet keeps trying to sing
out on the hilltop, but he's lost
                his tongue.
The taste of spoiled elegies rises again in his mouth,
as though he'd been fed
                the livers of infected birds at dusk.

Translated by Len Roberts and Miklós Horváth

The Nook Was Fine for Me

The nook was fine for me, the mattressed couch,
the hat-covered lamplight
above indented beds,
it was fine for me to have a creaky sleep.

The Moon, like a delayed fear of death,
would often arrive,
making the walls, the walking-clock's shadow, the window frame
        grow,
but it was fine even to be superstitiously afraid.

Snow was falling in Paris, hail in Zámoly, and on the mountain
        sides
of Georgia the blood of eagles poured into the valley;
in every defeat I was a stranger, and in every mourning,
but it was fine even to be a stranger on earth.

And it was fine to walk here in the light of kind eyes,
as it was fine for that slim, radiant man
of Nazareth, too, marching into the City
on an unkempt, Palm-Sunday donkey.

Drums rumbled for him in the sheep bells' quiver
like an epileptic soldier –
I have been shaken like that by the perishable bodies of my lovers,
when again and again the night awakened me to them.

Their groins were scorching, scalding,
just like the Jerusalem sand,
yet I have never thought of a rosemary-easy redemption,
but instead, of long-haired warm rains even today,

that come, say goodbye, see the trains
off or the tormenting wars of nerves.
The Sun comes out in their wake like immortality,
and snails set out slowly in the grass towards infinity.

Translated by Len Roberts and József Horváth

Night Journey in Germany

Darkness, wind. Down the Elbe
   some huge, shapeless cargo slowly floats.
     Perhaps a vast sack.
      Perhaps a ship.
Perhaps a lost, stray mountain after an earthquake.

Outside, the night is cold,
   the water's cold,
     like totalitarian states.

All the train's rushing iron is also cold.

Withdrawn into the compartment's nook,
   with downcast eyes I'm passing alongside
     Germany's wounds.

Can you see me now, dead men's eyes,
   shooting by on the riverside?
Can you see me, bone-citizens, smoke-souls?
I should roar, like one who, after forty years,
   now wakes from among the ruins
     to the scream of red-hot beams tumbling from the sky,
and I should beat the train's window with my fist,
that the past may pass, but
      beneath my skin
        there's the memory of all the meanness
          the war bequeathed us,
here, here, like a snake in the bowl of sweets.

Bloody little skirts: front-line poppies
   and church towers shot in the head
     lie on their backs, staring at me from the ground.
And yet my hands in my lap
   do not budge for them,

my throat does not open,
as though someone had stuffed
   velvet or roses
      into my mouth.

In the countryside all around
   darkness stands in indistinct mounds.
Trees, posts, terrible-eyed eagles from empty space
      meld into it,
and my dim, passing shadow melds into it, too.

Down the river,
   that shapeless spirit of darkness floats along.
      Perhaps a swollen sack.
         Perhaps a ship.
Perhaps a lost, stray mountain after an earthquake.

Farewell to Finland

Blue-gray clouds over Finland –
I keep retreating from under them, I say farewell.
Lines of poems slam behind me, mixed
with gulls and a sudden shower's raindrops.
What a September guard of honor!
It's easy to imagine: here, too, I could have met my death.
Leaning against the Rock Church's wall
I heard a clicking clock ticking
and the artery on Orpheus's temple, the one that cannot be
         stemmed.
I knew: I, too, was not allowed to look back any more:
let those innumerable women go about blond, untroubled,
         in sunshine to the groin,
         on Mannerheim Avenue;
let their hands smell sweet of early, green apples,
as long as the hand can smell sweet.
I leave, anyway, almost on tiptoe,
the polar light sitting coolly on the back of my neck,
like the silence of a postponed sentence.
This is how I lose my towns, countries one after the other,
the old route of boats toward the church of waters,
the waters, too. But the sea,
like the winter war's grayed veteran,
begins to sing behind me,
hoarsely, wildly – to me and to the colossal Sun.

It Will Remain My Living Memory

I'm here with you
    and right now it's good to be with you.
A butterfly's on the stone, on its wings the burning eyes of a
        peacock:
perhaps the billboard of summer,
or perhaps of your eyes.

Your body murmurs quietly beside me,
    as though a radio played lowly.
Your breathing's received by grass-antennas.
And a grass-herd of horses rushes toward you,
and the green flood of a hundred-acre wheat field from the hill,
and the fantasy of our being swept away
still pleases me now, as it always has.

I'll see you here and there in the villages,
    on writers' evenings, or beneath the bunned linden trees.
Cries and long curses flow from the theater,
but you'll run away
from every tale there as well,
and by the side of unknown men
you'll follow the crazed, frenzied sounds of May.

Already I feel it: I will have to pulse with the pain that you *were*,
and that you won't lie beside me anymore on the lake shore, in the
        hill grass,
and that it won't be me in your dreams
who will brush gray ladybirds off your body.

It will be good for me to watch a long time
the inviting bout of your beautiful breasts:
it will remain my living memory,
my model for every death.

People, Boughs

This day is filled with silence,
the world is filled with silence,
of mean silence, heavy silence,
as though a mute cuckoo nestled itself in my ear.
In the night, metallic trucks vainly swish,
secret terrorists getting ready for bloodshed
vainly shoot at mannequins:
the deafness of a box-like universe lurks in hearing's corridors.
The iron balls are also blunt. The dreams. The trains.
Forests soundlessly flutter: tattered
owls stuck on pitchforks.
Maybe I should fall in love with someone again,
with her breath,
the clamor of her clogs in the hallway,
and listen to her hair crackling as she combs it.
Meanwhile a year would pass,
two would pass,
and the sounds would return to me,
just like the darkly gliding swallows from Africa,
the sound of plates,
the sound of countries,
of rains kicking the sill,
the shoulder-cracking of spring from beneath the clouds'
        Beethoven-hair,
and the small leaf sounds
would whisper once more in my ear: we were and we shall be
        again:
people, boughs, sweet tongues rustling.

Translated by Len Roberts and László Vértes

Prophecy

The last spring shall come, the last summer, too,
before their fall, but no judgement, again, shall be passed.
The guilty ones shall sneak shiftily from the rooms,
from beneath the glass chandeliers imitating the sky,
into the open, among the trees,
and they shall blend with the rheumatic shadows.
In the parks, crickets,
at the feet of prophesying statues,
retching drunks. No one asks anything.
The faces of the ravaged shall be more harrowed than the
        criminals'.

You, Hungry for the Sun

(During the film shooting of "Drumfire"*)

What could you have said
to the dying men?
What could you have said to them there,
on the improvised war-strawbed?
Gauze in the corner,
wadding,
iodine,
bloody medals,
and outside, in the weedy garden, wolf's milk,
sand-flower
and Don-tulips,
and above the trench-filled spring fields,
low-flying bullets whizzing about
like insect-hunting swallows.
What could you have said
to them there, in the surging
frontline-cracking,
in the mine-stink?
That you are heroes, boys enrolled as angels,
and your peony-big wounds
will help the mother country to heal?
That from the water of home wells
your faces, wandering in the depths, will stare up
at the women drawing water,
and after you're gone, the summer will ache?
Ache? Or burn?
And big hayforks of straw
will cloud the sky for your sake?
Or that, in the lone line of poplars,
a chasm will open, there, where you laughed?
What could you have said to them, you of all men,
who, joining forces with even the cringing mud,

is always begging
for life's mercy?
Even now a radish snaps between your teeth,
and you want to walk away, to dash off like a deserter,
a lap of flowers luring you into the afternoon.
What could you have said to them,
you, hungry for the Sun, hungry for a life that never ends.

* "Drumfire" (Pergőtűz) is a film about the World War II battle of the Don-Bend in Russia, during which nearly an entire Hungarian army, about two-hundred thousand men, was annihilated by the Russian army. Csoóri, with Sándor Sára, wrote the film's script.

Dozing on the Train

The train's rocking me, I close my eyes,
a tottering row of trees remains inside,
a lake, a puddle, a barren dirt road
and the pockmarked patron saint of a ditch's bank.
And some leaf-like thing, greenly, also floats
     between earth and sky,
but it will never again land on the ground.

All aggravation dies slowly away
from the landscape and from me, too. The chronic
memory of violence, like the froth
from the lips of mad dogs, whitely frays.
Click, clack – the wheels are running to infinity with me,
     and I leave behind what the warring body
brings upon me daily: the blackmailing present.

Is this a waking dream? A play rehearsal
before death or after death? Above the summer, hands float
and swaying bell ropes also.
Nothing touches my temple
that has touched it to this day. She who cried, now cries far away,
     and she who undressed for me in warm rains
now undresses far away.

I can hear crickets stirring in withered,
distant grass, and the drought-stricken snap
of a stork's beak. This would be enough for me as a last sound,
enough for a hundred-day dream. Click, clack – the wheels
are running to infinity with me,
     and plains keep coming, swishing faster and faster,
ditchbanks stretching longer and longer.

Translated by Len Roberts and László Vértes

The Day Has Passed

The day has passed. This is easy to say.
Exhausted birds nestle close to God
and even my heart, this harnessed
draft horse, will rest, perhaps.
This is easy to say.

The day has passed. And nothing has passed:
for a long time the distant dead look
today, still, from under the rubble,
as if I had died in the street fight instead of them
and the victors now trampled over me.

The day has passed and nothing has passed:
feeble glimmerings on the ridge of early
evening sky and in the cool eyes idling in the street
and the moldering woods' green reflection
in the fathomless pupils.

This is the hour when the harrowed of the world
cry out in one pained voice upon the earth
and under tons of dirt. Then the sweetened
evening coffee begins to tremble in my hand
and the wind stirs the roots of my thinning hair.

The day has passed and nothing has passed
regardless of how perishable we are, here,
inside. In the beginning dark the breast
of a woman who died young used to hover, moonlike, before me,
and yet, now, in her place, I see only the jaded, thick-bodied
acacia racemes.

Translated by Len Roberts and László Vértes

Confession to the City

So much wind-blown garbage in the streets,
so many empty, vagabond faces
    and smothering smoke-streaks beneath the sky of the city!
And so many leached loves behind the walls!
But when passions change to green
   for a few seconds, like traffic lights at crossings,
the harnessed, leafy branches and rains thrust forward,
    lace-curtains drop from above
      and a gleaming madness rushes
        along the streetcar's tracks,
it whistles and whines, like the falsetto
       shriek of the flute.

I love you, I love you not . . . I've been tearing
your calendar's pages, City, for thirty years.
    I wander your streets,
      not knowing where I'm going.
Everything here is nearer to hand, to the body,
nearer to pleasure, nearer to murder.
From the dragon-throats of water boilers
      flames flash to my face, as in the legend,
and down below, in the underground sewers,
   the never-ending filth continually gushes.
City, am I yours? Or am I just
   your prisoner?

I desert you often, deny you, and yet yearn to be back
where fires now, too, sprawl
      like exhausted draft animals
        on the earth,
and a hedgehog roams in the garden, the primitive world's
      confidant,

but its velvety stirring is suddenly sundered
   by your hundred-thousand windows, your irons creaking,
and your fair, neurotic women forlornly shrieking,
and instantly I am there, with them again,
in the mirrored elevator's rising glitter,
             in the subway's hair-drifting draft,
multiplied by your myriad glances
and by my madness. If you don't let me stay with you,
             only a forest, perhaps, will think of me,
                 and death, leaning his elbows against the Moon,
and the world won't call for me in its hour of need,
it won't send word for me, expect me, send music after me
from which I might learn immortality. You tremble
   excitingly on my thin, white skin,
like beans on a shivering drum. Will you be engulfed by smoke?
Earthquake? The rambling fire-roses' rank growth? Even though
             I betray you, City, with you I shall stay.

Translated by Len Roberts and József Horváth

I Have to Look Long

I have to look long and kiss long
        to remember her body as it was just a day ago.
Her dark hair walks before me like a first-day widow;
I have to look long at her hair's color to see her once more.

She walks in rooms with me where I had been happy
        with another; pictures on the walls, screams in the walls,
and a flock of homeless, wild geese flies in the window
as if the mute ceiling itself also recalled.

But what's past is, for her, already the other world.
        An eternal full moon in the green of her eyes,
the eternal present, and a shivering plain of moss.

I'm standing face-to-face with her: I have to look long, long,
        to tear her off the relief of the snow-covered town,
to make the blood in her face, in her little finger, abruptly start.

                                        Translated by Len Roberts and Gábor Törő

A Thin, Black Band

Since I don't wake with her,
since I don't sit at the table to have dinner with her,
since death flowed into my laughing mouth
and I am caught between the rains,
as between the slats of the iron fence in my childhood days:
I can see a thin, black band wavering for a long time
before my eyes.
It comes closer, vanishes, once again rises,
as if an eye's swaying bloodshot vein hypnotized
me from morning till night.

I can see it, too, among the museum's massive columns
in the slanted, falling sunshine,
before the January statues' snow-mouths,
and near women's faces in the market, in the street,
standing on the escalator of the subway.
America fades away within me, the Great Lakes' light,
like when the lamp is turned off.
Startled, I look about, and haltingly I begin to believe
that the dead, too, are fickle,
and they won't stop their secret game
once, while living, they've started it.

The wind whirls, whirls upon the lean docks,
tips hats and roofs,
lures water from the middle of the Danube aloft,
and that black marvel dances there, there too, about
the prancing waterspout,
it draws my eyes, lures them after it,
like a strand of black hair that cannot be caught.

Translated by Len Roberts and Tibor Tengerdi

Apparition

The lake under the hill faintly whitens,
   like a toppled tombstone in the sun.
     To its right, a grove-like cluster of trees.
And among the trees, in a sackcloth shirt,
   a shaven-headed girl kneels
       and plays the violin lonesomely.
Flustered, blue butterflies flit about her shoulders.
I'm pushing a bicycle in the shaggy grass
   and stop to listen:
maybe a film's being shot about the angel-slaughtering times?
maybe a torn soul's talking with his secret God?
Or do geranium-scented St. Joans still arise
    today from the dust?
Her violin wails, as when a strip of skin
is torn from a living martyr's body,
it wails, like a falcon tumbled into a stake
     on a flowery vineyard hill.
I start toward her with a throbbing throat
  and my hands slowly begin to bleed:
oh, am I a man, after all,
   who is also capable of miracles?
My hands are on the handlebars, my head is in the sky, and
        butterflies
   drink from my blood,
making me lighter, like someone the sinners,
and madmen as well, can love:
my chest is full of chamomile-tremble, full of beetle-hum,
wild millet thrums my bicycle's taut spokes.

Summer, with Halo

A hornet flies into my room,
angel of June,
turning the curtain yellow,
and the room's four walls;
and just as wheat fields and woods walk
in front of the sky's glass window,
so summer, naked to the waist,
struts back and forth before my mirror.
Around her head, the clay hill's glitter,
the birds' halo, and your face's,
    washed from the dust and death
by the June shower.
Out there a tree, and a throbbing engine,
an airplane whistling from the other world –
oh, the big journeys are behind me,
somewhere, like you;
only this painful turning
remains, with the hornet and summer,
the gold flowing and cooling about me
with a dim, earthly glimmer.

Translated by Len Roberts and László Vértes

May Beetles

By day, too, the May beetles flit about the vineyard on the hill,
    they sing around the swelling cherry trees
like hungover high school students around Nagyerdo.
With my boned body
    I totter with them, too, in the air;
my sunken village may be seen from here,
my child-sole's lacy print in the dust,
and lizards that sit higher up on the limestone covered with moss,
eagles on the needlegrass mountain meadow,
and like the May Procession saints:
ox heads and horse heads from the past
    gather around me in a vast circle,
their eyes pure green stone,
    pure resin-brown,
we hum, dizzy, as though the carousel
of an age-old church festival twirled us;
from the burst eye of a whirling peony,
north and south, east and west
may be seen here,
all the conquering pains
    which tore me away from here.
Just whirl me around, May beetles,
    lure me up above the world,
it's good to know who I was,
it's good to know who I am —
so many May leaves press tremendously beneath me,
as if the world were still my forest,
my ray-filled forest, my vast, trackless May forest.

For the Seventh Day

I write this swishing poem for you,
    come soon if you can,
    don't wait until tomorrow night.
For the seventh day I've been staring at the stone–dead
    sandhills
from this bleak hotel, and at the bored little forest.
    A huge crow eats the snow in it,
patters, hawks, then soars away aslant,
northward. As if a black lump of flesh
tore out of me, taking wing.
I don't want to stare, alone, at the clock anymore,
at the bread, the knife, the body's
  abruptly risen, dark craters.
Some irrepressible, earthly whisper
  is about to speak with my mouth again,
    and I don't want
to have faith in myself alone anymore.
Come soon if you can, a cold wind blows here
    at the border of the country;
my hands are cold without you,
    like the hands of a soldier standing sentry duty.

Memories of November

The crows are knots of mist
    behind the thick, black boughs,
  and when they soar up: dark ghost-gloves.
  Maybe my death keeps frightening me again with them
    in this heart-twisting November?
    Or is it just playing with me
      like a drunk Gypsy with a puppy?
I can hear the rain patter on the nearby hospital roof,
    though it's only about to rain,
  I can hear it on windows, on cars of trains,
    I can hear it on the wing of a plane forced low
      over the Bahamas in sixty-one.
The blue, the yellow, the cherry-red coral islands,
    like the submarine sanctuary-candles,
  gleamed up to my face then,
as if the world had wanted me to live and to remember,
    and together with the big, soggy eagles,
      to find my way out of the storm's dead end
      even with a sheet-white face.
I didn't know the sky, where I was,
    I didn't know a single lightning, a drop of rain,
      but I knew what I liked:
    the slow gliding before the horizon
  and the uncertainty of the ocean, as now, the uncertainty of my
        body.
I watch some bit of sky glide
      in the empty space behind the boughs:
      it can be, perhaps, one of my memories, like the eagles,
        the rains,
        the sanctuary-candles,
      one of my memories, like death.

The Wood Embers Cast Light upon the Snow Outside

I'm stuck here again in the horseshoe valley.
The snow's banked around me, and it's been days now I haven't
        seen a man.
Only crows lurk about my cabin
   and the fox hallucinating in the nights.

What I desired, the winter now provides:
I can be on my own at last, and I can stare for hours
        at the forest, at the hillside,
   at the skeleton of nothing, or the reflection
of my cracked nail up in the tinny sky.

Big white bones also float on the Danube,
I can watch them, as though in a moving picture show . . .

And oh, ancients, forefathers, my ancestors,
you twinge suddenly within me
        under the walnut tree overladen with snow.
As though a wolf chased a herd of wild swans toward you:
   the wind carries the snow over you, the wind carries the snow.

Carries it into the well, and into the window,
on the roads, too, before your eyes.
        The storm, in a ghost shroud, splits wood
at the chopping-block, its nimble axe claps
   and white chips flit toward the sky.

And the chimney hums, the haystacks hiss,
a horse in the stable harshly neighs,
        its raspy voice cleaving into you:
it swoops upon you that, until Spring,
   neither God nor the newspapers can get through.

But I will! I will, through time, too!
Under the light blue beams
   I'll be there in the footrags' steam;
together with you, I'll shell golden corn
         and the cob's poverty.

   Will I be your guest, your son? Or just
the future's fugitive? A scot-free goblin
   who demands wine from your wine, and learns a world by
         spying on your mouth?

Your baked apple was better than Eden's,
       man will winter on its taste till death.

   Let a great snow storm: tons of celestial threads;
I will visit your place until night:
       the glow of your wood embers casts light upon the
       snow outside.

Translated by Len Roberts and Gábor Törő

A Drop of Blood on the Ground

The cat crunches the pigeon's bones,
    he's lustfully crunching, then turning his head,
but his eyes stare fixedly into nothingness
even from above the bloody shreds.
Only predatory Autumn can stare at us this way,
        with such a yellow lynx-gaze.

And look there: there's a drop of blood on the ground, too,
    a little purple leaf plopping from a tree,
and in a moment another one, a third, and farther, there,
under the horizon, the red block of an entire butcher's woods.
It's best for us to slip away from here,
        to give no evidence about the cat, nor the blood.

Besides, there are too many signs of death in our lives,
    too many memories of breaking
and of mangled chests. Come, maybe the destroying angels
don't know the secret lovers' way yet;
October's infantrymen-crickets carouse there,
        and honey, nut, and blackthorn offer themselves to exiles.

Sunshine and the Black, Night Bramble

I always bustled about you,
   you, sleepless,
      restless-eyed woman,
   you, gracefully lying, wavy southland.
At any time I can see through the nights,
      as far as your big breasts.

So this is carnal love, lechery
   whirling you into hells – iron-priests and severe virgins
      would have squawked in days of old.
   This, this! – I, too, nod afterwards,
now, when I can smell your groin's fragrance
      in the June forest's body scent.

Stubborn soldiers leaving for the front
   were buried under as much hair,
      under as many last nights
   as you wrapped me with –
Perhaps you considered me: I was a soldier, too,
      and your bullet-proof embraces would be a shield.

You never became my ringed fiancée,
   nor a quince souvenir upon my carved armoire –
      nevertheless, it was you with whom
   the October rains could weep so well.
Your long, soaked afternoons were like those
      when Chopin played the piano in Paris for himself.

Your opening, swollen lips spread your body
   wide before me, like a camouflaged door opened
      before an infamous fugitive;

sunshine and the black, night bramble swept
into you with me. When I was in you,
    I was the world's fireseed.

This early summer forest is full of trembling,
    full of springy smiles now, too,
        from your strolling memory.
    I can see: you stop, sit down upon a stone.
Your taut, beautiful breasts flirt with the entire sky,
      and the taste of your opening lips is sweet bramble on my
        lips.

Translated by Len Roberts and Tamás Juhász

Green Twig in My Hand

Spring will turn frothy again
   like the mouth of the ever-singing bird,
and grass will grow around the mounds of earth,
     but you will not smile anymore
at anything that will be alive.

I will take a green twig to you, chicky catkin,
     beaming cowslips from beneath the mill-dam,
God's glance gleaming on them
     and the glance of the first bug crawling out into the world,
but you, drawing aside, just stare at the wall.

Who knows whether I will survive my incurable embarrassment,
   but I still want to remember even this last look in your eyes,
these eyes that burn black holes:
     sterile chalk-dust drifts into them
as though smashed Carthage's dust reached you only now.

I do not think death is more talented than me.
   I do not think death could take you away from me.
I can see myself in you as though I were sitting in a beautiful
          wound:
   green twig in my hand, and behind me, oh behind me,
vast spaces: all around me the otherworld darkening.

Translated by Len Roberts and Claudia Zimmerman

43

Postponed Nightmare

I'm sitting in the sunshine,
    getting warm as the rocks
        after a rough, rheumatic winter.
    At my ankle a small wind stirs in the grass,
your breath from down below, perhaps.

They say I wept months for you.
    That may be; I can't recollect.
        On either side of me the nights blackened
    and horses reared with blood-frothed mouths,
as they do when a shell bursts among them.

And trains and cities and a flock
    of crows plummeting headfirst
        and the skidding, burning wrecks after
    midnight on America's roads,
where I waited, mid-dream, for a crash.

I yelled to you: come, there is a renewal
    in my madness, my pain that is
        greater than pain: the severed
    head, the arm, fly toward you
and our eyes meet again—

I'm sitting in the sunshine,
    getting warm as the rocks.
        A winter's postponed nightmare cries out in my bones.
    At my ankle a small wind stirs in the grass,
your breath from down below, perhaps.

Translated by Len Roberts and László Vértes

No Kin of Yours, Just a Friend

Poland: lightning-struck Christ statue,
    the July sunlight patrols
        your blackening wounds
and flies again kiss your bones.

I sulk for you,
    as though I, too, lay felled in some stinking pantry
        and stared at a lone carnation
in the mirror of bransoup.

I could be Rákoczi*, your little lord, without a horse,
    a student leaning against the walls of your church,
a linden-scented soldier who arrives home
        only now from a long war,
his dead ones in the ground, unclothed,
and above him stunned bugs, swallows
and the smoke-hats of ruined cities shooting against the sky –
but who am I to you, great-faithed, pale country?
No kin of yours, just a friend, a nettled Hungarian
    who loafs about your emblazoned streets in a huckleberry-
             tasting noon,
who, even in his sorrow,
looks for a lover among your daughters,
for he wants to touch,
he wants to embrace,
to rave with you to leaf- and sunbeam-music,
to endure the putrid beetroot's stink for hours
    in front of the grocer's,
to endure the unendurable,
standing in line for the wildest hope.

                             (July, 1981)

* Ferenc Rákoczi II, Prince of Transylvania. He was in exile in Poland when he was declared by the Hungarians to be the leader of a revolt against the Hapsburg rule in the years 1703-1711. The phrase, "Rákoczi, little lord," is taken from a folk ballad.

Translated by Len Roberts and László Vértes

You're Rising and Vanishing

The road slowly rises
with sudden bends up the hill.
Clouds rush over your shoulder to the North.
The countryside is so hungry for mercy, and so tense,
like a train with soldiers that starts for the front.
You don't even know where you turn: in
a strange country or your torn homeland.
Bush leads to bush and you stare at each branch,
each leaf dipped in red.
He who has torn himself forever from another body's warmth
learns with you to say a final farewell.
You're rising and vanishing high above. The coppery
taste of cooled songs in your mouth,
like that of old coins placed on the eyes of the dead.

Translated by Len Roberts and László Vértes

I Saw Your Face

(in memory of István Bibó*)

Potato sack and long loden coat —
for days these things of yours have come to my mind,
and the ruthlessly long mornings
when one waits for his turn in the market's cabbage smelliness
and life is like a rusting thresher
in a distant barnyard.

For a long time I did not know who you were:
perhaps a worn-out widower
                             I had thought for months
with some sympathy,
perhaps a pensioned heart-case, above whom
now the boom of the Mártirok Road bells lingers.
Then the name. Your name. Your handshake.
Then the glasses gliding from the cobblestones up to the sky.
Then the Hungarian Old Testament sins in half-words
there on the street corner and the New Testament filth.
You are coughing from cold memories
but at once you smile, too,
like fate's well-bred one and history's
last gentleman, who awkwardly kisses the hand
of Antigone passing through centuries
and sits down beside even the common graves of the abandoned
            dead,
sinlessly assuming the living's
sin.

How often I thought that I: could be you as well,
Hungarian to the very end, since desperate to the very end, self-
            devouring,
who stares anxiously in the honey-bearing acacia grove
and even near the rippling mouths of women:

have the eagles not invaded his hands
and have the axes not chopped up his smile?

I saw your face, alone, like mine now
this morning
and I also saw your eyes:
calm martyrs gaze thus, parting,
at a chestnut tree that's blossoming,
the way you could gaze into others and yourself.

A potato sack and a long loden coat –
for days these things of yours have come to my mind,
and the ruthlessly long mornings
when man could still redeem himself in your name,
but he just stares at the ground in his shame.

* István Bibó: Hungarian political philosopher and politician who was imprisoned for
his beliefs and later released.

Translated by Len Roberts and László Vértes

Sky, Earth, Brass Doorhandle

Dreams, crazy night. I start up.
Clumsily, I keep snatching at words,
like someone tumbling into water snatches at foam, at dark
          floating drift-wood.
Sky, earth, brass doorhandle – I murmur instead of prayer
just to myself
and I suddenly see my mother behind the words:
she is opening the brass-handled kitchen door,
a pail of water in her hand, a pear-tree blossom in the water,
and the entire brittle sky, unscratched.
A tiny bee crosses the threshold with her
in a transparent gold shirt.

Oh, reflecting dreams and words: how could I believe
I do not stand before my young mother even now,
in there, on the kitchen tile?

Psalm in the Forest

I breathe, I walk among the trees —
this is now my history.

The forest, like an unpublishable manuscript.
With dark strokes, the birds
draw lines through the leaves.
Branch-burst,
then silence,
splitting membrane walls.

A spot of rust on the moss.
A passing season nears.

The ants' friendly factories
will be plundered by rains:
soldiers of autumn's military maneuvers.

Once again I must learn to be cold,
to smuggle the sun and future under the ground.

And life lives through me again
even when shamelessly shoved aside —
from my memories the grass once more will turn green,
and the trees turn muddy.

Where I tread: rocks wince
in the earth,
like the bony hands of my dead,
so I won't be left alone in Time
and my body, too, might feel its own company.

Thorns flip toward me,
as if trained knives
whizzed.
Patience, patience—I whisper:
in the place of the bird's eye, a clotting drop of blood.

Questions to Carriers of the Dead

Who are you? What are you dragging?
Are you hauling the Unknown Dead toward the cemetery?
The untimely victim of speeding?

I saw the dent of the man's body that had clapped
against the stonewall in the nightfall,
I saw his blood and time's blood stream together.
So simple was this haphazard, clumsy last judgment,
as when a dew-drenched calf is killed.

And what is that wreck you have left?
The car's knotted dream of itself?
Hell's junk? Iron-trash?
I feel an itchiness beginning slowly under my skin,
the unswingable hand's eternity here on the ditch-bank,
and among the stones the silence of butterflies and excrement.

Translated by Len Roberts and László Vértes

She Wanted to Say Something More

She wanted to say something more,
something more I should know about,
perhaps about the snow,
about her long hair falling out in tufts,
perhaps about the miserable molehills in the Matra
she had dreamt of so much,
perhaps about her hand's weight,
perhaps if there would be a war again,
perhaps about the knives, her veiled wounds;
about the creaking windows beneath the hospital window,

perhaps about the splitting spring which would waft,
without her, a willow leaf around my face,
perhaps that I should die with her,
perhaps about my muddy shoes in a churchyard too large to trek
            throughout.

I watched her eyes, her mouth,
the dimness pressing in her body,
her hand's path to my hand,
but that sentence was nowhere already,
nowhere was that word split with pity,
only her final smile shone on me from among the pillows,
her final, earthly smile.

Esztergom Summer

I lay with you there on the bare floor
in the makeshift log cabin –
it was summer, the daisies and bushy creeper's
tiny lamps shone through the planks in the evening.
If anyone had seen you maimed and fallen,
I might have killed him,
since you could laugh at your fading wounds,
cry, that you were still living,
that you could walk within an arm's reach of the overladen plum
            trees,
you could be a tear in the eyes of a country
when it thought of its long-lost mountains.
At every waking the wind swung
a chime from Esztergom;
I can see you now, too, as you clutch
at the early peal
and swing yourself high above the hills.

Translated by Len Roberts and Anita Sényi

The Long Winter's Psalm

This winter is long, doesn't ever want to end.
Even the year-old pigeons have been crippled by it.
They patter, matted, on the rooftops
        like the lumberyard's disabled night watchman.

Shrove Tuesday has passed, Ash Wednesday has passed,
but in place of the bloomy catkin's unfolding, it snows instead,
even though the old snow still
        lies there under the gouty bushes.

Among the rubbish of newspapers, tin-boxes, beheaded
rubber dolls, my eyes stroll. I imagine
my heart holding such ruins as this.
        I'm filled with memories of bridges razed in war.

The doorknobs, the hands, the streets are cold.
Before our watchful eyes
only a frost-stricken ferry floats back and forth
        with a lone crow on its ice-splintered deck.

I still remember every spring, every summer.
I harbor enough birdsong under my pillow to last a thousand
                years,
but I would be mad, a fool in drawers
        to trust just my memories.

God has fallen asleep. The ancient hope sleeps.
Imitating the eyes of a fairy, winter's big, electric heaters

only make me lazy. Under my skin
    I must urge myself to a fresh desire.

I hear the winter's immigrants pattering
down the ages: curse and cough choked
                      in the chest.
And some blast of heat slaps me: protesting breaths rise,
    fiery, from the old mouths, billowing before my eyes.

Translated by Len Roberts and László Vértes

Winter's Voice Has Softened

Winter's voice has softened in the trees.
The forest also no longer creaks
like an overloaded farm cart.
The branch tips are growing fleshy: my fingers'
                    glistening relatives,
they are swelling, pattering excitedly in
                    the blueness of March;
if they could speak, all their words
                    would be pure moisture,
pure splashing, the noise of a distant water-waltz,
just as I am a streaming that has started
to pour from the mountain as well,
a Christ-like freshness above the stony meadow.
I offer my skin to a thrush,
                    let it nip me,
for it's time already
that nothing should hurt.

I am about to live, to play,
I don't know who still remembers my old name?
The beech, the linden, the butterflying
branch of the cherry still remember,
they come across the mountain to meet me, as in my childhood
          days,
they twirl the wind around them in a hoop,
winter's voice softened in them,
softened.

Translated by Len Roberts and Claudia Zimmerman

We Were Good, Good and Obedient

(for my generation)

We were good, good and obedient,
like the little boys hung with cherries in the promenade,
    we didn't trample the grass and didn't undermine
    the dahlias planted in the park.
We were good, good and obedient:
we hissed out even in our sleep
    for the stray dogs kicked in the back,
    but we avoided the eyes of cowering men
    as though they were puddles of blood at an accident.
We were good, good and obedient,
we saw Georgia's cliffs in brave sunlight,
    we drank its wine,
    we saw the Black Sea trudging home at night
and the ancient gods left without mouths,
    and, with velvet stomachs, we ate dinner out of sheer spite.
Mozart, standing on his cold star, played music for us
    to the horse-radished rump of beef.
We were good, good and obedient,
the wind blew, the years swayed to the side with us,
    like an airplane circling slowly over
        a lit city,
    the fine, drifting ashes of the advertisements' fires
        and the world's fires shot up to us,
    the epaulets of generals hurrying to receptions glowed yellow,
but we watched, instead, with chattering teeth, Jancso's★
        paradisiacal
            women on the movie screen
    and the perverse little panties they hung on the crosses
        of graves.
We were good, good and obedient,
misfortune stepped, in her skirt, over
    our aching nose-bones,

through us the past was brought to pass,
but we still fondled the memory of a trumpet-resounding ball
    from the time of the war,
as though stuffed pink sacks
    had taken our places, dreaming, those nights.

* Miklós Jancso, famous Hungarian film director and producer, who presented naked
women in his films during the 1960s and 1970s, causing some public outcries.

Translated by Len Roberts and László Vértes

I Go Near You to Die

Midnight. The tender elders grow
    in the darkness also;
I'm walking between them toward your cemetery,
tipsy and shabby,
        like the poets of old.

At this hour in mawkish novels the Moon wanders
    with a diamond violin,
and bats ramble close to the ground.
I hear only a sick thrush whimpering
      at the bottom of a bush,
    raving in its dream.

I cry, mourn for you, stop, then start to sing.
    I watch the stars galloping at breakneck speed,
and I must always think of you, you who
      have become unthinkable,
like the world's afternoon and the air's wound
      around my mouth.

A word, a whisper says this in the dark: you were feverishly hot.
    Another, this: you are the memory of this dirt road
      on which I grope,
  and the unredeemable dust will keep
your feet's lecherous tracks.

Words, words. The heartbeats of nothingness
    in me: words which go to die,
as I, too, go to die near you
      in the evenings,
along the elder-lined road, in the heavy dust.

A Dawn Story

Day's lightening, with red streaks.
This night of mine was the devil's again.
Standing in water up to my ankles, I dug a big ditch.
From its muddy yellow walls
moldy tatters stuck raggedly out:
a shirt sleeve and a coat
and, crooked, a dead man's brimmed hat.

No, this is no dream – the vein throbbed above my temple:
something has happened here, something even I don't know
            about,
some pointless, delirious sin:
people were killed here as a circus spectacle;
look, there's the mangled magic wand and a gouged
eye in the breast pocket!

Away with the spade,
    away with the uprooted magic wand, away with the ditch
and I'm running: where's a living creature who will help me
dig up the leveled field?
The road's empty,
    the bridge,
        in the forest empty swings sway
from tall trees,
the sky is cut from above by an iron-toothed saw,
big blue chunks of heaven
are thudding into clearings
and smoke and flames shoot up from where they've fallen,
but there's not a man anywhere,
not a whimpering dog,
only scattered tires, like dark, flat jellyfish –
I stop short: this country is not my country anymore,
beyond the forest, reeds are reddening,
past them, endless water, thundering nothing.

Translated by Len Roberts and László Vértes

Part Two

(1973 - 1982)

I Believed Then

I've never desired anything more
than that green evening again on the village fringe:
I lay, face down, in the May Grass with you,
the skirt drawn slightly up your thigh,
and the unsuspecting May beetles flitted over us,
doomed guests of the universe,
and I believed then the world
would take me back again,
the earth, the trees, the delusions that survived the winter,
the world – tired of its losses, would yet take me back.

Translated by Len Roberts and László Vértes

The Poppy Clatters at Night

The poppy clatters at night:
with it, my conscience starts up: after all, I have abandoned you.
It's been summer ever since, it's been summer for years
        and you live alone
               alone in the house of cages.
No one says to you: adjust your small shawl,
for the world may come for you yet.
You drink when you should cry,
you drink when your name-day arrives,
you drink when you see darkened thighs
        entwined in a secret bed
and the rains hang before you like infinity's fraying threads.

It's all the same now, what happened and how:
I have squandered carelessly my eternity
that I stole from you;
and my family now: jackknife and bread,
country of green trees
around my head
and the sweetness of a woman engaged to death –
I am with them,
        if the elder-scent seeks me where you live,
or the secret policeman disguised as a window washer,
I am with them, and you are now only my widow.

Translated by Len Roberts and László Vértes

European Summer

Light,
        light
                for days now.
Raging summer wherever I go.
The memory of blazing straw-stacks in my eyes,
Rome burning in an infernal fire,
flaming red popes,
                parched statue-kings.

Europe: a sunflower drooping to the ground,
a hornet, yellowly, flies around it,
Gothic lace jams on the horizon,
hills of alum closing war
wounds: the remnants of flashing, crystalline
mourning above the undressing towns.
Oven-mouth breathes on me
from the West,
concrete-mouth breathes on me from the East. Lightning
wires burn,
                ornamental hubcaps,
                    mirrors,
                        heated spokes,
and from inside, too, as though platinum-thoughts embedded
in bones burned me:
I'm choking, I'm fleeing
up to the North, to Finland's
shady corners,
where water, long left to itself,
                sings in water,
                    forest stands behind forest,
                    the Moon stands behind the Sun,
and from behind the Moon
the animals can hear
the loud beating of my heart.

Darkly from the Darkness

Coming from your place, the ditch-bank covered with frost,
all of Rákoskeresztúr's crows following me home,
cursed crew, they haggle like Gypsies around my car,
they're squealing, overtaking me, they don't want me to think of
        you.

But if they knew I left my wristwatch beside your bed today too,
they'd stop this hurly-burly wedding party, this rude joke,
since even my faded wrist makes me remember you till
        tomorrow,
just like the news at noon, and the books in which last-century's
        snow unceasingly falls,

and even in the museum's timeless garden, in front of the stone-
        coffins' sculptured women,
I can see you stooping: you're straightening the sheet at home,
your hip leaning forward, your hair pouring down onto the bed—
and I can't escape your African buttocks even during my daily
        rushing.

And cormorants, equatorial falcons, eagles could come upon me,
I'd see even through the slits of wings when you unfasten your
        skirt,
and from behind even the danse macabre of big birds your eyes
        would blacken toward me,
as from the darkness you raise them darkly.

You Enter the Moment

You enter the moment, as though the train pulled
        into a foreign country without you.
A window-flash greets you from somewhere up high.
        and a hand, a face, a doorhandle,
          a mauve nightshirt flutters before you
and sinks quickly into time.
A sill and dust are left for you to remember, and swallows
        that flitter
          like the scraps of a shredded card
            of condolence in the morning.
You are close to falling between two clouds
        into an abyss.

Somewhere, the bells are ringing. Maybe in your head.
The blood rides swiftly on the chime of the bells toward
      the whoring nothingness.
You are alive, alive, yes, alive — towers, alleys,
black shadows prove it,
your momentary heartbeat in the gurgle
        of the fountain on Margaret Island;
you are alive, alive, yes, alive — with your strong hands
          you might as well wring the necks
        of the pet peacocks there behind the wire fence,
as peoples and races have butchered each other throughout the
        ages.

But even if the moment is yours — the present isn't!
        it kisses your forehead and then walks out on you,
sits on a stone, soars up, circles, moves into a dark pigeon;
you stare after it, as after a craving that's been embodied,
and unshoutable words tremble throughout your mouth.

Postponement

Still not today. Today there is still no way I can hide
     away into the earth. Today from the garden
        a wasp-sonata still slips into the house
  and by nightfall even love's nest
      fills with screams.

Still not today. Today still no way.
     Today I may still open
        the door for guests:
     for wind, for star, and for the dill's scent
        that comes before the lurking, lazy, little death.

Still not today. Today still no way.
     Today I still must live and fear
        that a train may run me down, water swallow me,
    or in the aged row of poplars
      I'll be given a bullet for the journey, just like
          the poets who are yet to go into the ground.

Still not today. Today still no way.
     Today it is I who see clearly for you,
        because I see myself: in the borrowed light
  of arms and unfriendly cities I loaf about,
        between my fingers a walnut leaf bleeding to death.

Still not today. Today still no way.
     Today my eye still peers out
        from a huge eye,
    as though I were watching from the sky's center
      my body's shadow being passed down among the
          summer trees.

Translated by Len Roberts and László Vértes

Belated Demonstration in a French Mining Town

(for Sándor Sára*)

The wind blows, all day the wind blows,
Saint Etienne's sparrows are cold,
they shiver even into this poem, with which
I accompany myself–
God of roads, snow clouds, snows,
so, you have dragged me even to this place!
I eat the cold orange in front of the Prefecture's stone palace,
I eat with the hundred-year-old mouths of Zola's poor.
This is a belated demonstration,
yet it is good to think: in the blue and red
neon butterflies' flutterings
I am now the indisputable hand here,
the mouth's eagerness,
the memory broken into bits with sticks;
I am the town's overgrown head:
I hear the police bullet thud from the long-dead,
I hear under the stones the trotting
of mine horses that have gone blind.

On the long, lit streets
I appear with all my pasts,
with all my poverty, all my songs–
My face grows threadbare near the store window's furs,
like a sack
in the light of fires which are for sale,
it grows old,
yet I bear a few victorious aches
toward the approaching night,
this stubborn body, chilled through
before the overheated bank-wombs,
like one who has come directly from under the earth,
from among the battered zinc basins and bones.

* Sándor Sára: Hungarian cinematographer and film producer who worked with
Sándor Csoóri's filmscripts in the 1960s and 1970s.

Translated by Len Roberts and László Vértes

Let the Timbrel Rattle

I'm growing sleepy over the poem,
over myself,
as though it were Sunday afternoon for weeks now,
as though I've been staring steadily
at the white of the sky's eye turned inside out.

Snow's about to fall, my phone to ring,
the pigeon grown stiff with cold is about
to fall off the tottering roof antenna,
and in the weary fancy of the void
this falling is now left unended.

I turn the radio on, the past,
the ceiling-lights of memories: let a green meadow
with tilting butterflies
rush toward me from beneath the Vértes Hill,
and a long whistle from behind Havana's red clouds.

I want life, a din, crying from several ages at the same time,
imperfection's awful uproar or anything else
that shames the eardrum;
adulterous bodies and countries,
so what is loved again should end only when the world ends.

I have no beard, no power, I'm not a would-be suicide,
but I'll invite the old tune of danse macabre,
let the timbrel rattle, the snappy bone-music begin,
I want to tremble, to shudder,
like the overworked horses.

October Tirades

Clouds slowly begin to stir,
leaves begin to stir,
the red-dye forest would also begin to stir in the sinewy trees.
                    X
Where, where are you off to, feet? This is the autumn river!
Where, where are you off to, feet? The mud chills my eyes,
the earth covers itself with soaked potato-sacks as well.
                    X
Once again I am searching for myself, but where should I look?
I enter gloomy rooms where I have been,
gloomy poems, a row of poplars without a roof,
I'm recognized everywhere by those who loved me, who saw me,
but they only remember my leaving.
                    X
Now they return from the big trips, after sickening
summer merriments,
those who rocked their wives' sun-glistening bellies
across Europe,
a rowdy, noisy crowd, accomplices of empty pits—

they stare at me, too, but they turn away.
                    X
A wind-tugged leaf glides in the place of my face,
a stiff eagle feather from a blackthorny sky.
                    X
Seeing my bones slide apart,
anyone might think I'm full of hate,
but I'm just tired,

tired, me, the one who always wanted more than his ingenious
            body:
to exist separately through the gleam of his eyes and his nails.
                        X
Where are you off to, feet? Every road's end is already known,
every clock stroke, every sky —
if only I could be a wild-flavored apple in the world's mouth that
            is opened so wide.

Translated by Len Roberts and Claudia Zimmerman

Somebody Consoles Me with a Poem

Can you hear it? Somebody's reading a poem to me over the
          telephone,
  he's consoling me for my dead,
    for myself,
      he's promising a snowfall on my forehead,
snow on our common resting place:
  on a bed, forests, beyond the skeletons of yesterday's flowers,
and healing silence in a gentle cellar,
    where cut plum-tree logs
      will burn, blazing,
there will be wine on the table,
    onion
      and bread,
otherworldly light gleaming from a sharp knife,
and on the timeless, white cellar wall
  an ant, separated from its army,
    marches toward future centuries.
Can you hear it? What he says, he says to you as well:
  with big, black wings
    don't flap into the night,
      into mourning, into soot,
you're not an angel, nor a condor,
you're a sweet country's sole dweller,
  you're mine even though you're condemned to death!
    Your bound hair tumbles down
every night to my wrist
and I turn toward the North Star
    together with your back—

Weapons may stare at us tomorrow, too,
our misled country with thistly eyes,
we will no longer need your mercy:
we've lived everything that is life,
    everything that is the worry of people who die too early—
Look: the promised snow is falling softly already,
    down to our footprints advancing in pairs.

Translated by Len Roberts and László Vértes

Prophesying about Your Time

For it shall come,
you'll see, it shall come,
before your fall, it shall come,
at the foot of the roughcast tenement walls it shall be morning
            again,
summer again,
a long day of curtained loins
and water will drench your linen shirt,
even the bones shall soak in water,
        they shall swim forward,
                backward, upward,
as if you were pillaging
the sea's crypt—

it shall come,
you'll see, it shall come,
even before your fall it shall come,
a low-flying pigeon
shall have its stomach stained with blood upon the rocks,
and the sky shall be filled with the trolley wires' orange sparks,
and on the hot boulevards
cars,
        words,
                shouts shall fly about
like balls of lead shot: caravans of lead shot,
and you'll walk among them
cloaked
with dust and smoke,
and in your swaying to one side is the challenge to death,
yet you shall be invulnerable then
because you'll remember nothing,
yet you shall be invulnerable then

because you've been evicted from your wounds—
Crazy! crazy!—the mouths shall hiss,
like water-splitting pipes
and from beneath the whiskered water-jets of sprinkling trucks
so shall the crusted concrete—
Crazy! crazy!—from the fashion plates' faces
twenty-thousand-year-old honey-smiles shall engulf you,
and there shall be ants in the store windows,
ants in the walking street's gray bed,
ants in the barracks-yard's unclosed eyes,
ants inside the kicked-apart clocks,
     they come,
        they go,
           they swarm,
with cogwheel wreaths
          they shall wreathe
          the emptiness,
it shall be magnificent,
               I tell you, it shall be magnificent,
because it is only you who can come after them,
you, who were able to wait
from the first to the second pain,
shifting from the red into the black,
and from black back,
and become incarnated every day,
to sweat,
       to split apart, to go on.

Translated by Len Roberts and Judit Vértes

Everyday History

To rise
and make fire in the stove,
in the brain after the reeling of the smoke,
in the ducts of the bones cold from sleeplessness,
and to seek the way to the hand,
from the hand to the drinking glass,
the remnants of yesterday's ashes in the hollows of the face,
perhaps a bird-blown windstorm will revive them yet,
and to wander
from one body to another,
and like nomadic kings: to seek the everyday motherland,
and, having found it
or not,
to spend the night in a single smile's tent,
and to walk in the Creation like a stranger,
to breathe in the dawn
poison of the trees,
the iron dust of the towns,
to go to all the wars,
to wear the lilac leaves around the neck
like a dogtag
and, understanding everything
and understanding nothing, to part with what I love
and rage for what I loved,
brazenly, like my own life's
hired man.

The Stranger

A man comes, knocks at the door, looking for lodging,
but like a robot he can only smile at the door handle,
at the yellow-blooming room–aerial.
I mutter: forgive us, but we have just lost someone,
we'd like to spend the night quietly with him,
talking to him beside the wine and plain bread,
and be together with the forest's murmur, which he used to hear.
He keeps nodding, but just stands there, lost in the midst of my
        sorrow,
although he, too, is the Earth's child.

Aiming Orb

Our clothes lie scattered on the floor. As though insolent
thieves had been at our place and had gone
off through the closed window, to behind the clouds.
I search for their footprints on the zigzag roofs, but
only the track-covering slime of the fog shines. Only
the redness of the attic-eyes.

Pigeons in the rainspout. Soaked, they walk up and down
in canvas-colored featherfrocks, like frontline fighters in the
                messengers'
trench. I can see clearly only the crown of their helmeted heads
through dawn's aiming-orb. Now, now the curving trigger!
Now, now the dazzle of spattering pigeon feathers!

Well, yes, it's useless to deny it: here skulks, here waits
in me, too, day after day, an unemployed murderer,
a tuned-up marksman. But you do not know
the trembling nostrils
because you see only my right eye when you turn toward me,
and my right eye is yours entirely:
it enters your cave-dark hair,
it lures the sun's first ray above your morning-after loins,
but my left eye, like the owl's, is motionless,
like the hammered nail head, motionless,
like the gun barrel, motionless.

Translated by Len Roberts and Claudia Zimmerman

Nobody's Land

You don't say a word,
I don't say a word, though we can see:
nobody's land keeps growing between us
and our nights are overgrown with weeds, like the cemetery.

If I had time for the pain,
if I had time for forgetting,
I would put on clothes like lead
and sink to the bottom of the lake,
but I must live here, where you, too, must live,
I must walk here, where you walk,
here I must silently leave the heaven of doorways behind,
where the noise of an iron handle is the grinding of teeth.

If it weren't for only one body that is given
to live with love and to survive it, too,
we would have begun to run long ago between the slender trees of
          another time,
and we would have torn our hands off one another like burning
          shirts,
and our mouths would have talked long with another sky,
they would have filled the nights breathing solace,
they would have squeezed spring and suffocating honey
from other bones.

It Is Only Myself I Haven't Seen

I saw walls in the dusk,
horned with shadows
of thin trees;
a river with its throat slit, bleeding to death alone;
pebble quarries in the sunlight, when the stones,
like lizard eggs, crack.
I saw the sea rock beneath the sky,
the swollen legs of the hanged.
I saw the war: from the dunghill bloody sheepheads
were watching the beaten soldiers.
I saw bright forests,
sunflower fields:
glittering like the Earth's medal.
I saw love: with an early green leaf
wiping the dirt off herself.
I saw finely-featured faces
staring in the mirror
and the mirrors dimmed.
It is only myself I haven't seen yet without you,
the unhoed gardens without your hands,
the wretched son of man without your tears,
only the world have I not seen yet, where my home
                                        might be,
if your eyes, left open, would let me go.

Translated by Len Roberts and Miklós Telbisz

Sea Gull-Line

I sit down here every day and this window does not
crack. Above the rails of the sumac, the eastern sky's
snow-filthy boundary stone.
    On the Danube ice-Ophelias float,
        mad drifts of whiteness.
In the clarity of winter who needs the strength
of my eyes? Who needs my breath: through the pores of the wall
the wind wildly sucks me out into the whirl of the street,
crookedly above myself, like a piece of shrapnel leaping away. I
           bump
into a harsh sea gull, I freeze to its wing.
Beggar of hoarfrost, fly me! At Carnival time,* let's make merry
in white, but don't you drop me into the places of the missing! I
don't want to keep freezing in the cold chairs
of the dead. Here they like the ones to be glorified,
they carry around the ones to be glorified.
They make their rotted tongues swim in formaldehyde.
I won't be the doorman to the needle's eye, the caretaker of the
        fatherlands!
I don't need the broom, the power, the key,
the commission; let them pin the bloody shirt of legends
up on the walnut tree! I lighten, glow red, change
back to dark, I fly headfirst into myself, competing
with the iron-turul** of the iron bridges, turning my time
into history, my rocking into plummeting, dragging
my body in a sea gull-line behind me, like smoke.

*Carnival time: A festival held on February 27-28, which celebrates the coming of
spring; participants usually wear masks.

**Iron-turul: mythical eagle of the ancient Hungarians.

Translated by Len Roberts and László Vértes

My Winter Kingdom

I cannot run on ten paths,
I cannot die ten deaths,
well, then, I'll wait for that special one
which sinks me to the depths.

Winter, my kingdom,
is a snowflake kingdom only;
my departing on a hundred paths:
a lone departure only.

Translated by Len Roberts and László Vértes

Cantata Profana

(in memory of Béla Bartók)

We did not go home today either,
we did not go home, boys.
In vain mother scoured the knives,
in vain she scrubbed
the knotty table.
In the mud of its blood,
with its neck slit,
in vain the goose wailed.

We did not send a word,
we did not write a line –
as if our hands had been swept away by a flood.
Easter is no longer Easter,
the swept house
no longer our house.

X

Who is that old man over there?
Sitting in front of the white wall's ghostly aura,
sitting in the cigarette smoke of the world's end.

His face is a crushed wicker basket.

He might be waiting for us,
looking for us,
wishing to see us
in the street beyond the window,
in his short-sighted life.

Don't look for us,
don't wait,

you, old man reeking of tobacco,
you, poor, doghouse-breasted one.
We are no longer your sons.
If the door opens, it's like a jacknife.
We would only rush upon you like a blast,
we would tremble by you
like an electrical current.
Plates and wine glasses
would crack,
and hair grown to our shoulders: roots of continents,
would weave through your stomach,
and you would become a hair-basket,
a hair-man,
a corpse which can be singed.*

*This reference to singeing probably alludes to the practise of burning the bristles of a
pig after it is slaughtered.

Translated by Len Roberts and Anita Sényi

Perhaps a Bullet

Perhaps the cold tap-water would be good,
perhaps coffee that tastes of everlasting life: let me shiver,
perhaps the crunching of the snowdrift shirt upon my skin,
bird-nails and iron filings on my eardrum,
perhaps the lewd hip-show of the woman across the street in the
         mornings,
the slow rocking of the ocean-going breasts beyond the window,
perhaps a brotherly elbow poking
between my ribs,
perhaps a bullet into the jamb.

I Would Let You Go, Call You Back

I would let you go,
call you back,
in a great water I would make your bed,
and being your tireless sailor
I would sail around you with my hands.
Where you would go,
I would follow.
It's summer,
I move out under the sky
to be the nomad of your love:
let the Sun shine like fate —
with my whole body
let me burn!

The inaccessible future
and tomorrow's dying desires give strength —
bullet-shower of wasps
would pierce my skull,
the world would take my blood,
yet I just smile,
because I see you.

I would let you go,
call you back —
a funeral procession of ants is surging,
I would shove you from their path.
Lifting you from the dust, I'd give you water,
I would bathe your wound with my words.
I would lie beside you,
and with your black hair
block out the world.

Translated by Len Roberts and Judit Vértes

After All

I have no one to talk to, still I say:
    I was a lucky dog, after all:
        my hands, like world–weary travelers,
could rest upon your face and upon your thighs.

The Smile of My Exile

There is nothing but this dawn hour,
steep, shadowless trees
and silence tuning these trees.
Only the neighboring pine forest, like a bombed railway station.
Only clouds, your swollen eyelids;
only the flooring planed from your breath,
sigh-thin plank;
the sinking island of your face,
the smile of my exile,
only the pain that I will cheat,
roads drenched with rain,
pools,
smooth stones.

Translated by Len Roberts and Miklós Horváth

Eyes

The crevices, the crevices,
my world's narrow windows,
keyholes, door-wounds, gaps,
someone always spied in through them,
to my wrist, to my bed,
and to the root of my dream where even I can't see anymore,
where the very first sour cherry bleeds
between my teeth and murderous graters
lie crooked in my throat –
and pit-a-pat: my friend's girl
crosses my scarlet threshold
between the rising walls – eyes in front of her, eyes behind her,
eyes, eyes: diver's and torpedo-eyes
in the deep waters connecting my cells,
eyes, eyes: clinging disk-eyes
on my back: whom do I leave behind tonight?
To whom did I hand my purple glass in the garden?
And the one who threw pig bristles on the flowers,
is he my fellow conspirator?

Eyes, eye-lensed, idle, fallen eyes
from behind the light-shelter of the lamps,
eyes, eye-lensed, idle, fallen eyes
on the street corner which breaks the wind –

as though I had to sleep in store windows,
as though I kissed in a meat stall.

Translated by Len Roberts and Claudia Zimmerman

This May Be Summer Already

This may be summer already:
radios play in the open windows
and the mare-maned hairdresser leans her elbows on the sill
beside her sunbathing fashion magazines,
the bitten tacking thread in her mouth, like the navel
cord of a child born with wings—
my face flits across her face, as though she'd already dreamed of
         me,
as though I'd stood in the abruptly opened doorway
with a blackthorn branch,
then a ruffled feather floats away in a daze before her eyes,
then a ship's trumpet-stack, silently,
then a chunk of blue sky, without a crease,
as, from the torture chambers, it can never be seen—
it may be summer,
summer indeed,
the heart-radar forecasting distant aluminum rain
and suspect love affairs
with a hoarse swan song.

Translated by Len Roberts and László Vértes

A Friend's Pleading Words to a Second Person

Before you should lose me
and cover me forever with loamy earth,
seek a pleasant, blessed day,
a pleasant day that lasts from morning to dusk:
draw me from the bedchambers of anger into your Pentecostal
   fields,
draw me from the scenes of deceitful games and the usual
   bloodsheds
into the thistles,
let my troubles gurgle in the sky's dikes,
and let me eat wild sorrel, not meat, that day,
and cherries and air,
and let the birds drum on black bark again;
my eardrum wants to rejoice,
my eye wants to shine through sealed pheasant eggs,
for even though I love your houses that lean against the sky,
your lamps that move in the dark, drifting away
like motorboats,
my life will end there, where the locust leaves
lie on the ground,
the ant forecasts earthquakes
and, dipped in the forest at the village fringe, I may belong to the
   wild again,
I may be the eyeball amplifying the drippings of the sap.

Translated by Len Roberts and Claudia Zimmerman

Message

Today the enemy stays away again,
far from our shoulder-pits, from the smell of our skin,
but sends a message from behind the lit woods:
we are defeated, we should not forget,
our hand is a hand stuck in rock,
we're on the ground, we're under the ground,
we are under the apron of the swamp,
in the rose garden of fossils below, deeper,
and we are not to move, not to breathe,
scoured wombs dazzling above us, like copper cauldrons,
down, even deeper,
down, beneath the floating driftwood's darkness,
backbones flattened!

Translated by Len Roberts, Miklós Telbisz and Gábor Törő

On the Third Day the Snow Began to Fall

The first day was good
        for me to forget about it all;
the second to remember it all.
And on the third day the snow began to fall
        and the misgiving was born
        that from this time onward it will always fall,
        from your forehead to your mouth,
        from your mouth to your loins,
        all along your body,
        all through my life.
The ceiling, the receiver will snow
        when I lift it,
the blurring sky of childhood, when I look back.
Even among the deadlocked trees and stacks
        only the snow's ghost roams,
        settles on the darkened fields,
        crowns those who escaped the war.
And then I knew I will never be alone,
this snowfall will escort me wherever I go,
sit down beside me on the train,
cross the sea with me,
in the night of smoldering tires and stifling cities
        it will call to me in my mother tongue
        and conquer a country for me,
        for it was you who wanted to
        conquer a country,
and when I have no homeland either, because I won't have the
        strength
to bear witness to it,
        I will lock myself up into this snowing,
        like one who puts on a white shirt,
        a white shirt on the last day.

Translated by Len Roberts, Miklós Telbisz and László Vértes

Part Three

(1 9 6 2 - 1 9 7 3)

Barbarous Prayer

Stone of unsmoothable folds,
rock of motherly light,
take me back to your womb.
My birth was a mistake;
it is the world I wanted to be:
at the same time, lion and root of the tree,
amorous animal, laughing snow,
the wind's essence and the height's
ink-blot trickling in all directions –
and yet, I've become a man lost in clouds,
ruler of one road only,
man with a star of ash,
and what I gather in myself
soon splits me apart, for it passes away
and only makes my longing grow . . .
Stone of unsmoothable folds,
rock of motherly light,
I'm standing before your womb's threshold.

Translated by Len Roberts and László Vértes

The Wind with Its Nerves

Here your hand turns blue
and here your cymbal-face claps to the ground.

There is no other age which would harbor you,
no other country which would give you a name:
here you are bound
by the nerves of the wind,
by the fog's cotton threads,
here you are welded with the final patience.

The sunken axle-trees of carts
turn this land
into spring,
into summer.
The hill studded with wine-stocks:
as if Saint Istvan's* crown remained here.

Listen to it,
space's jostling din:
the neigh of colt, the clatter of hoof.
And earthenware plates cracking like bones.
A thousand years shatter into bits with them:
László Hunyadi's** shoulder, nape—
You may run in front of the immaculate Notre Dame,
but even from its writhing devil-throats that filthy spillage gushes,
the misery of your land.

Like a scrap of shrapnel rambling in your flesh,
you carry its ruins within yourself;
and if your wounding binds you here,

your healing binds you here, too.
Lie down in the mud,
into the harrow-rough thornbed,
laugh or snarl –
You can embrace somewhere else as well,
but only here does the right to kill remain for you.

* Saint Istvan: Saint Stephen (977-1038), also known as Stephen I. He reigned as king from 1000 A.D. During W.W. II his crown and other regalia were taken from Hungary by the Germans. After the war, they were transported to the United States. They were returned to Hungary in 1977.

** László Hunyadi (1433-1457): the elder son of the famous Hungarian general, János Hunyadi, in the wars against the Turks; he was executed on the basis of false charges.

Translated by Len Roberts and Anette Marta

What Do You Envy Me

What do you envy me, animals:
dogs glowing under my window,
horses looming beside the carriage-pole?
My pointed shoes, my shirt's pearl buttons?
My tie, which, like a long, summer morning,
turns the chalk-dust age red-hot?
What do you envy me, dirty beasts:
regular customers of mud-pubs at the village's end?
My bed, which I'll die in?

Stars are stones set into the river—
I'm skipping on them,
maybe I'll reach some opposite bank.

Do you envy this daily skipping?
Or that I can devour you?

The smudge of your blood: an icon on the wall.

Your moan, your squeal: executing music—

What do you envy me, animals?
Love, because it split me in two
and nailed me on the town gate?
The goodness,
the sin,
the fence of whitewashed human faces
being erected around me?
And the supreme evil, that I can also fear myself?
This poem?
These loaned words,
which, like a division of tanks, start thundering

and carry me to latent wars?
The body's threatening silence,
with which it clothes the storm?
The splinter of infinity
and my mind's finite hymns?
My cells' final argument,
which I can draw, like a tin-knife, on death?

This Day

One day with you,
one day the madness again:
the dusk of your room and your body,
its boundlessness and silence.

Your uncovered mouth and nothing else—
outside woodbine sparkles:
a black-and-blue mark in the sky.

It's a bold hope to love like this,
to be born for your mouth, your breast,
to blend with the sky and the earth.

The summer, like blood, clots,
like empires, it collapses:
flower-ruins,
leaf-dead
gather around us as gentle dirt.

Don't be afraid, I'm not afraid, this day
embalms your bed,
your hand, your silence,
and I'm lying beside you even
when dream carries me home,
when I have no more words,
only these:
There is wind,
it is evening.

When I Touch You

Why should I write poems
when I can be with you?
Just to adorn time
and babble?
Instead I seize the Sun
like a bowling ball
and knock down
the horizon's forests
again and again for your sake,
into a heap,
a single pile.

Why should I write poems
when I can be with you?
Your breasts are more beautiful than the most surprising simile,
and your mouth more beautiful than the barest rhyme.
It's summer,
your hand burns like a magnifying glass,
and your belly turns the sand on the lake's
shore hot.

Birds and trains make their way
toward your place.
Now and then, when the smoke dresses you for an instant,
my eyes hurriedly undress you again –
I don't even know, why do I want to see you constantly?
If you were a bed of reeds: I'd gaze at the reeds,
and if earth: the earth.

Why should I write poems
when I can be with you?
The words turn empty, like the cottages in fall,

they perish, like people,
but when I touch you,
the touch remains immortal:
it doesn't wish to become the future,
nor memory –
why should I write poems
when I can be yours entirely?
Your legs',
your hands',
your breath's.

Translated by Len Roberts and László Vértes

Hide the Miracle

Everything's so plain and planned.
Hide the miracle, so I might love it!
Like wedge-headed locusts, explanations
restlessly devour the world.

Nothing makes my heart leap anymore,
so I look at the sky-rending miracles
as at a woman dressed in a sack, an elephant playing with a ball,
impatient, flustered, just for an instant

and I'm always looking for a madman in myself,
a saintfrancis
   talking to machines and continents:
a fanatic with an incurable mouth, who suffers
if he has no dangerous secret, no dream that can't be prevented,
for thus he has no hope, either — sunshine's just pouring down on
   him,
as on enthralled grass, as on fearful stone faces.

Translated by Len Roberts and László Vértes

Light-Blindness

Sparrows crash into large, yellow walls.
Already this is summer: the month of light-blindness –
slip away from your mother! Ophelia
is missing from beside the strolling Hamlets.

Out onto the roads! Into your hair's thickness!
Through your eyes! Wading above cricket-fragments
and machines, into the lap of your melon-red chasm!
High above, clouds, your clouds: drifting mummy cambrics.

Translated by Len Roberts and Anette Marta

The Snow Is Storming

The snow is storming,
now I want to talk with you —
geese are migrating on the road: refugees of the war
bearing the sack of January on their backs.

After nine-hundred days and nine-hundred nights
I, too, should fly back home,
but an army of crows throngs
on the wooden bridge at the village's end —

this is still love's Don-Bend.*

X

I hear a slamming door: distant cannon roar;
I have no path: neither backward nor forward,
just this winter, just this homelessness.

X

I have been unfaithful to you according to the people's law
and I'll die for you according to my own.

X

The snow is storming,
now I want to talk with you,
like the poor,
like the prisoners-of-war.

* Don-Bend: The River Don in the Soviet Union, where approximately two-hundred
thousand soldiers of the Hungarian Army were killed during a World War II battle.

Maple Leaf

Autumn's wreck, maple leaf,
you are a severed hand,
a shriveled palm.
Yesterday you still waved to the boys
who ran to fetch milk,
and today
you clang into my waking.
You turn time yellow
as a living
face.
Whose word do you bring?
What do you want?
Would you give me the handshake of the wind?
No need to console me: I live my life.
The summer's wreckage
slowly drifts to the other shore —
you, maple leaf, are stranded.

The Sun clasps a cloud-accordion,
but tugs at it
in vain,
it remains silent.

You, too, will have to submit to the silence,
and you, too, will get stuck in it.

Countries are smoldering in as many as three directions,
like burnt-back garden weeds,
and jungle-corpses' hands are clattering.
No remembrance for them,
how should you get any?
We, human beings, live in a time other than the Earth's,

to other seasons we give birth,
other sympathies,
other fears –

you turn my face yellow,
maple leaf.

Translated by Len Roberts and Gabór Törő

I Smear Mud on My Face

Days, weeks . . .
        The starry sky: sand-glass,
a hand turning it, my time growing less.
I smear mud on my face: pass by me
if we should meet in the movies, on a hilltop, in a street.

I've waited in vain:
        I'm not who I used to be,
the one who saw the birth of trees,
the dead swimming in blood,
and imagined that some day he'd be left to himself, alone
with the world, as with his pocket mirror.

That day never came, nor that silence,
only the wind: love overturning the basket
of my chest;
only the gangs of dusk came:
drunken hunters across the fields;
only the frosting-mouthed speakers,
only the paperbag-headed monsters;
newsboys waving continents in war,
musicians who kept tuning cannon-barrel trumpets.

Only the crossroads jamming under the eyelids,
the innocent dead, companions with their traded heads,
my mistakes,
my shames, like a long funeral procession,
the hands of homeland and family calling me to account.
The blind eyes of stone roses stick onto my eyes—
blindly I, too, look into myself like this.
Everything is one: my life and my death,
only he who is to bear this is absent.

Translated by Len Roberts and László Vértes

So It Should Not Be Dark

The bold bridges can still be seen,
and the impersonal row of trees
on the concrete bank:
the afternoon's falling snow on the faces of children
running home can still be seen.

But the water is covered with soot
and the body's night is falling, too.

I think of those who may be destroyed,
who are not shielded by a dream.
Silence whizzes into their room like a bullet,
and loneliness like the news of death.

I think of those who may be destroyed,
the earth is full of them:
no armies protect them, no rose arbors, no scented shirts,
not money's silver fences,
not love.

And in vain they die, for in vain they were born.

I think of those who may be destroyed,
only a hand would be needed, so they should have a homeland,
only another body, so it should not be dark.

Translated by Len Roberts and László Vértes

About the Translator

Len Roberts is the author of four books of poetry, the last of which, *Black Wings,* was selected for the National Poetry Series in 1989. His fifth collection, *Dangerous Angels,* will be published by Copper Beech Press in spring 1993. Roberts has received a Guggenheim Fellowship in Poetry and two National Endowment for the Arts Awards in Poetry, in addition to other awards. He was a Fulbright Scholar to Hungary for the 1988–89 academic year, during which time he translated most of these poems. He lives in Hellertown, Pennsylvania with his wife and three children.

CPSIA information can be obtained
at www.ICGtesting.com
Printed in the USA
JSHW021411080822
28991JS00001B/1